EXPLORE 360°
POMPEII

PETER CHRISP

WITH ILLUSTRATIONS BY
SOMCHITH VONGPRACHANH

BARRON'S

Creative Director: Darren Jordan
Executive Editor: Selina Wood
3-D Artist: Somchith Vongprachanh
Texture Artist: Drew McGovern
3-D Statue Artist: Guido Salimbeni
Design: Darren Jordan
CD-Rom: Jonah Gouin
Picture Research: Steve Behan
Production: Charlotte Cade

Historical consultant: Dr. Hannah Platts

First edition for the United States, its territories and dependencies, and Canada published in 2015 by Barron's Educational Series, Inc.

All inquiries should be addressed to:
Barron's Educational Series, Inc.
250 Wireless Boulevard
Hauppauge, NY 11788
www.barronseduc.com

ISBN: 978-0-7641-6766-9

Library of Congress Control Number: 2014940635

Date of Manufacture: December 2014
Manufactured by: RR Donnelly, Dongguan, China

Product conforms to all applicable CPSC and CPSIA 2008 standards.
No lead or phthalate hazard.

Printed in China
9 8 7 6 5 4 3 2 1

PICTURE CREDITS

The publishers would like to thank the following sources for their kind permission to reproduce the pictures in this book.

Key: t = top, b = bottom, l = left, r = right and c = center

4. The Art Archive/De Agostini Picture Library/L. Pedicini, 4-5. Bridgeman Images/De Agostini Picture Library 5l. Corbis/Scott S. Warren/ National Geographic Society, 5cr. Topfoto/HIP, 6. The Art Archive/Musée d'Orsay Paris/Gianni Dagli Orti, 6bl. Flickr/Karl, 6tr Bridgeman Images/Leemage/Private Collection, 7tl. The Art Archive/Kharbine-Tapabor/Coll. S. Kakou, 7tr. Topfoto, 7. Getty Images/O. Louis Mazzatenta/National Geographic, 8bl. The Art Archive/Manuel Cohen, 8-9. Bridgeman Images/De Agostini Picture Library/L. Romano, 9tr. Bridgeman Images/De Agostini Picture Library/Foglia, 9cr. Bridgeman Images/Bibliotheque Historique de la Ville de Paris, Paris, France/ Archives Charmet, 10bl. The Art Archive/Araldo De Luca, 11tr. Bridgeman Images/De Agostini Picture Library/L. Romano, 12bl. The Art Archive/Musée Archéologique Naples/Collection Dagli Orti, 14. Bridgeman Images/Museo Archeologico Nazionale, Naples, Italy, 15. Corbis/Araldo de Luca, 16l. Corbis/Mimmo Jodice, 16-17. The Art Archive/Araldo De Luca, 17t. Akg-Images, 17b. Topfoto, 18cl. The Art Archive/Gianni Dagli Orti, 18tc. The Art Archive/Musée Archéologique Naples/Gianni Dagli Orti, 18bc. Bridgeman Images/De Agostini Picture Library/L. Pedicini, 19bc. The Art Archive/Musée Archéologique Naples/Collection Dagli Orti, 19t. Photo Scala, Florence - courtesy of the Ministero Beni e Att. Culturali, 19br. © Jackie and Bob Dunn/www.pompeiiinpictures.com, 20bl & 20-21. The Art Archive/DeA Picture Library/L. Pedicini, 21tr. Alamy/Prisma Archivo, 22bl. Alamy/Isolated Objects, 23cr. Alamy/Biblelandpictures.com, 23br. Getty Images/ De Agostini, 24. Alamy/Tony Lilley, 24c. Alamy/The Art Archive, 24bl. Alamy/Andrew Bargery, 25r. Corbis/ Araldo de Luca, 25bc. Alamy/ Ian Townsley, 26bl. Akg-images/De Agostini Picture Lib./L. Pedicini, 27t. Getty Images/Werner Forman/Universal Images Group, 27b. © Daniele Florio, 28l. & 29tr. The Art Archive/DeA Picture Library/L. Pedicini, 28-29 & 29c. Bridgeman Images/De Agostini Picture Library, 30. Bridgeman Images/Museo della Civilta Romana, Rome, Italy, 31t. Bridgeman Images/Musee des Antiquites Nationales, St. Germain-en-Laye, France/Giraudon, 31b. Bridgeman Images/Museo Archeologico Nazionale, Naples, Italy/De Agostini Picture Library, 32. Akg- Images/Hervé Champollion, 34. The Art Archive/Gianni Dagli Orti, 35tr. The Art Archive/Manuel Cohen, 39. Bridgeman Images/Mondadori Electa, 39br. Bridgeman Images/Museum of London, UK, 40bl. Akg-Images/Bildarchiv Steffens, 40br. Topfoto/Alinari Archive, 40-41. & 41br. Topfoto/ HIP, 42-43. Bridgeman Images/De Agostini Picture Library/L. Romano, 43c. The Art Archive/Musée Archéologique Naples/Collection Dagli Orti, 43tr. Akg-Images/Bildarchiv Steffens, 43br. Bridgeman Images/Museo Archeologico Nazionale, Naples, Italy, 44. The Art Archive/ Bibliothèque des Arts Décoratifs Paris/Gianni Dagli Orti, 45t. Shutterstock.com, 45b. Private Collection, 46t. The Art Archive/Musée Archéologique Naples/Gianni Dagli Orti, 46. iStockphoto.com, 47t. The Art Archive/Gianni Dagli Orti, 47b. Akg-Images/Gilles Mermet, 47c. Campana Collection, 48. Shutterstock.com

Every effort has been made to acknowledge correctly and contact the source and/or copyright holder of each picture, and Carlton Books Limited apologizes for any unintentional errors or omissions, which will be corrected in future editions of this book.

EXPLORE 360° POMPEII

Pompeii is an ancient Roman city in Southern Italy buried by a disastrous volcanic eruption on August 24–25, 79 CE. The deep layer of volcanic ash that covered Pompeii also preserved it. It is as if the whole city was frozen in time.

We have recreated the most remarkable buildings of Pompeii using ultrarealistic 3D graphics. Now you can visit the city as it was before the eruption, and see the buildings as they were two thousand years ago, when Romans still lived and worked in them. These amazing new views of Pompeii are so real that you won't believe your eyes!

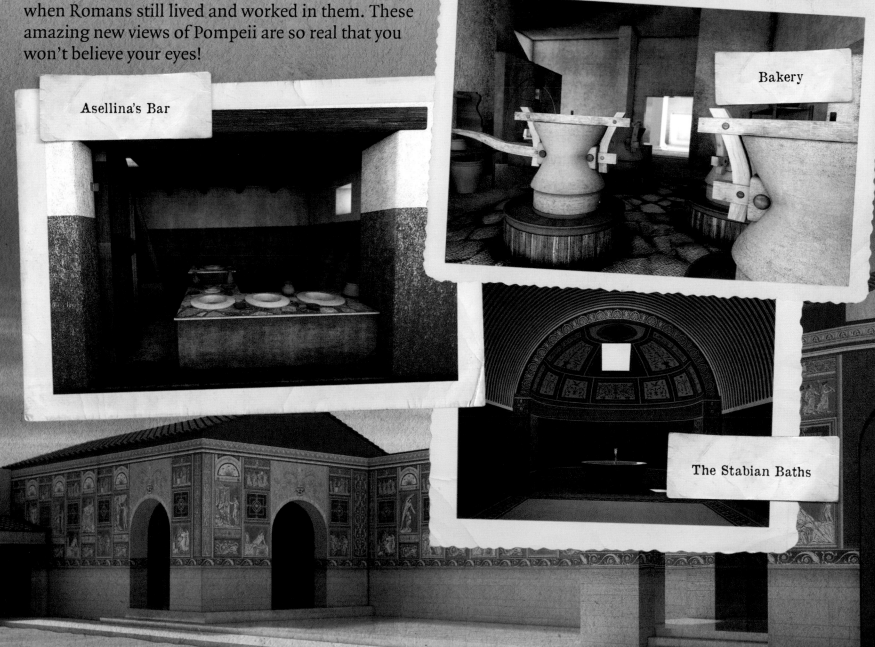

The House of the Faun

Asellina's Bar

Bakery

The Stabian Baths

THE VOLCANO ERUPTS!

Pompeii was a prosperous city founded in the 6th century BCE under the shadow of a great volcano, Mount Vesuvius. It had a population of 8,000–12,000 people, and covered about .27 square miles (.68 sq km). In 79 CE, the people of Pompeii felt no danger from Vesuvius, which had not erupted for 700 years. But that was about to change.

"DARKNESS FELL, NOT THE DARK OF A MOONLESS OR CLOUDY NIGHT, BUT AS IF THE LAMP HAD BEEN PUT OUT IN A CLOSED ROOM. YOU COULD HEAR THE SHRIEKS OF WOMEN, THE WAILING OF INFANTS, AND THE SHOUTING OF MEN."

Pliny the Younger, eyewitness

THE DAY OF THE ERUPTION

At midday on August 24, 79 CE, Mount Vesuvius erupted, sending a great column of gas, rocks, and ash 18.5 miles (30 km) into the air. According to an eyewitness, Pliny the Younger, the column looked like a pine tree, which rose into the sky on a very long trunk, from which branches spread out at the top.

MOUNT VESUVIUS

A wall painting (below) shows Vesuvius as it looked before the eruption. Its fertile sides were covered with vines, used to make wine. During the eruption, the peak of the mountain was blown away, leaving two great craters.

In this painting from the House of the Centenary at Pompeii, Bacchus, the Roman god of wine, stands beside Vesuvius.

RAINING ASH

For the next twenty hours, there was a steady fall of ash and lapilli (small stones), carried south by the wind. This fell on Pompeii at a rate of 6 inches (15 cm) an hour. During this period, many of the people of Pompeii were able to flee with their most precious belongings.

The nearby town of Herculaneum was covered in a layer of ash which was 66 feet (20 m) thick. You can still see the wall of ash surrounding the excavated buildings.

PYROCLASTIC FLOW

Around 4 A.M. on August 25, the column of smoke fell back on itself, sending a fast moving current of hot gas and ash, called a pyroclastic flow, down the mountainside. This was the first of six surges, which overwhelmed Pompeii and neighboring towns. Pompeii was hit by the fourth surge, around 8 A.M., which reached temperatures of 212–752°F (100–400°C). It instantly killed everybody remaining in the city.

THE LAST DAYS OF POMPEII

Vesuvius had another big eruption in 1828, witnessed by the Russian artist Karl Briullov, who was visiting Pompeii at the time. He was inspired to paint "The Last Days of Pompeii" (right). Several other painters have also depicted the scene. Briullov's painting inspired a popular novel with the same title by Edward Bulwer-Lytton.

Briullov depicted a scene with terrified people and buildings toppling around them. The sky is lit up by flames from the volcano and a flash of lightning.

"The Eruption of Vesuvius, August 24, 79 AD" by French painter Pierre Henri de Valenciennes, 1813.

A REMARKABLE DISCOVERY

For centuries, Pompeii and the other towns buried by the volcano were largely forgotten, as olive groves and vineyards covered them. The memory of Pompeii only lived on in the name "La Civita" (the city), given by locals to the area, which they knew to be a good source of stone for building.

Guiseppe Fiorelli

EARLY DISCOVERIES

In 1709, workmen digging a well discovered marble from the theatre at the town of Herculaneum. The theatre was found to contain many beautiful bronze and marble statues of Roman dignitaries. This started a treasure hunt, as the theatre was stripped of its statues.

EXCAVATING POMPEII

From 1748, formal excavations of Pompeii began. The most important work was done by Guiseppe Fiorelli, director of Naples Museum from 1863–75. He cleared many of the streets, and divided the site up into numbered regions, blocks, and doorways. Unlike earlier excavators, who stripped the buildings of valuables, Fiorelli tried to ensure that objects were left in their original position in the houses.

This is a statue of Livia, wife of Augustus, the first Roman emperor, from the theatre of Herculaneum.

This 1865 painting by Edouard Alexandre Sain shows women helping in Fiorelli's excavations, carrying baskets of earth.

CASTS OF VICTIMS

Fiorelli is best known for his plaster casts of the dead of Pompeii. Their bodies had decayed, leaving spaces in the hardened ash. Fiorelli found that, by pumping plaster into the spaces, he could make casts of the dead. These casts caused a sensation when they were first exhibited.

This cast shows a man leaning on his elbow in the moment of death.

HERCULANEUM

The neighboring town of Herculaneum was also excavated by Fiorelli. Many items that were destroyed in Pompeii were preserved here by carbonization (partial burning). These include a complete library of 2,000 Roman scrolls, wooden furniture, and cloth.

This cast shows a guard dog still wearing its collar. The dog was chained to the wall and unable to escape.

"NOTHING COULD BE MORE STRIKING THAN THE SPECTACLE. THEY ARE NOT STATUES, BUT CORPSES, MOULDED BY VESUVIUS; THE SKELETONS ARE STILL THERE, IN THOSE CASINGS OF PLASTER."

Marc Monnier,
The Wonders of Pompeii, 1870

This remarkably well-preserved, carbonized wooden cradle was discovered in Herculaneum.

STREETS AND BLOCKS

Pompeii was divided into walled blocks called insulae (islands). Each insula included houses, workshops, apartments, and shops. Some insulae might have up to a dozen houses. One insula was composed of only a single large house, the House of the Faun. In the city, rich and poor lived side by side.

"O WALLS, YOU HAVE HELD UP SO MANY BORING WRITINGS THAT I AM AMAZED THAT YOU HAVE NOT ALREADY COLLAPSED IN RUIN."

Graffito from Pompeii

This fountain shows Abundantia, who represented abundance and wealth. She holds a horn of plenty.

STREET NAMES
The streets of Pompeii have names given by the archaeologists who excavated them. The longest is the Via dell'Abbondanza (Abundance), named after the figure of a Abundantia, found on a street fountain. We do not know what, if any, names the streets originally had.

The Via dell'Abbondanza stretches across Pompeii from west to east.

VISITING A ROMAN HOUSE

The biggest house in Pompeii is called the House of the Faun, after a bronze statue of a dancing faun found here. It covers 32,400 square feet (3,000 sq m), and is richly decorated with paintings and mosaics. The house dates from the early 2nd century BCE, so its decoration would have been quite old-fashioned in 79 CE.

PATRONS AND CLIENTS

Every morning, the owner of a large house, such as the House of Faun, would receive visitors. They would come to pay their respects and ask him for favors. He was known as their patron, and they were called his clients. On entering, visitors would step over a mosaic on the floor, saying "Have" (greetings).

This mosaic from the entrance to another house shows a snarling guard dog and the words "Cave Canem" (Beware of the Dog).

CAVE CANEM

FLOOR MOSAICS

The House of the Faun had a hall called an exedra, with a floor mosaic showing Alexander the Great of Macedon in battle with King Darius III of Persia. This is thought to be a copy of a famous 3rd century BCE painting, now lost, by the Greek artist Philoxenos. The mosaic measures 109 by 205 inches (272 by 513 cm).

You can see Alexander (left) charging toward King Darius (center), who looks back at him in terror.

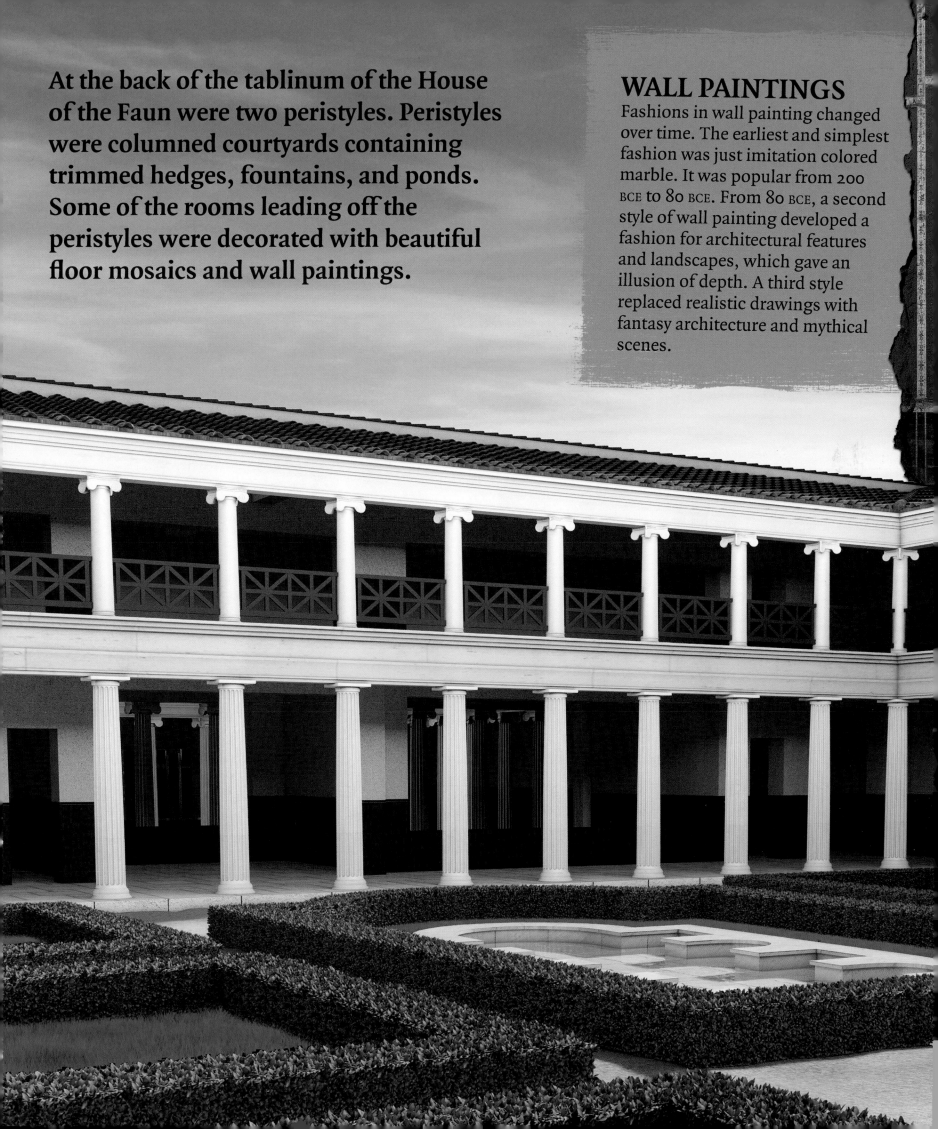

At the back of the tablinum of the House of the Faun were two peristyles. Peristyles were columned courtyards containing trimmed hedges, fountains, and ponds. Some of the rooms leading off the peristyles were decorated with beautiful floor mosaics and wall paintings.

WALL PAINTINGS

Fashions in wall painting changed over time. The earliest and simplest fashion was just imitation colored marble. It was popular from 200 BCE to 80 BCE. From 80 BCE, a second style of wall painting developed a fashion for architectural features and landscapes, which gave an illusion of depth. A third style replaced realistic drawings with fantasy architecture and mythical scenes.

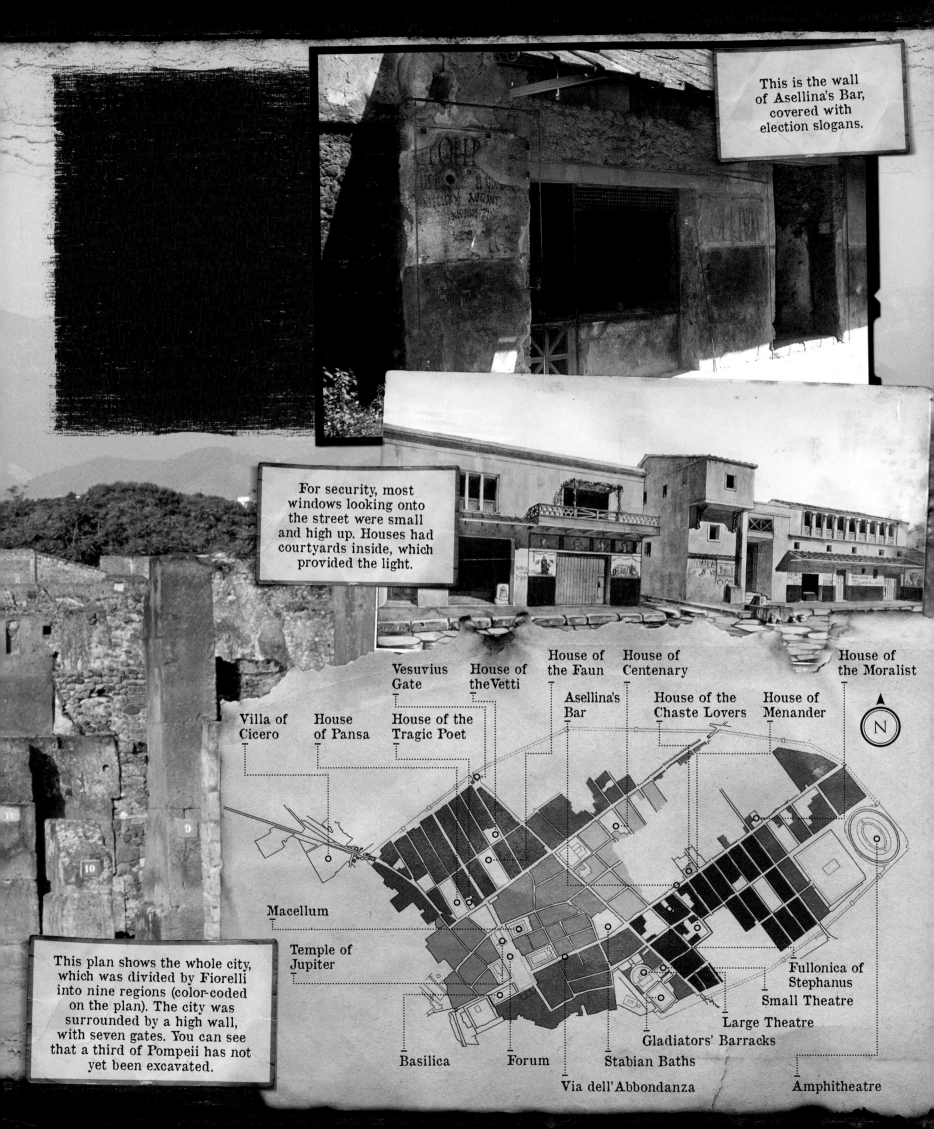

This is the wall of Asellina's Bar, covered with election slogans.

For security, most windows looking onto the street were small and high up. Houses had courtyards inside, which provided the light.

This plan shows the whole city, which was divided by Fiorelli into nine regions (color-coded on the plan). The city was surrounded by a high wall, with seven gates. You can see that a third of Pompeii has not yet been excavated.

N

Villa of Cicero

House of Pansa

Vesuvius Gate

House of the Tragic Poet

House of the Vetti

House of the Faun

House of Centenary

House of the Moralist

Asellina's Bar

House of the Chaste Lovers

House of Menander

Macellum

Temple of Jupiter

Fullonica of Stephanus

Small Theatre

Large Theatre

Gladiators' Barracks

Basilica

Forum

Stabian Baths

Via dell'Abbondanza

Amphitheatre

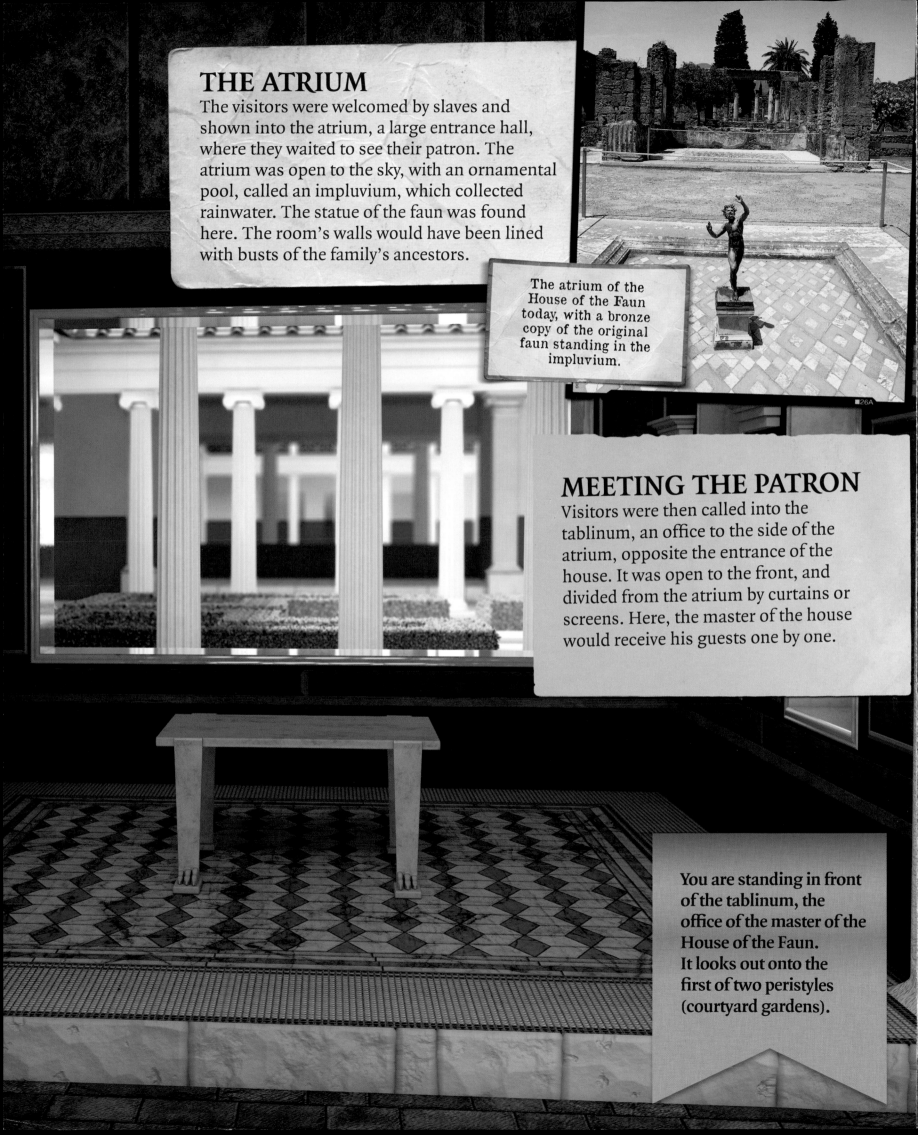

THE ATRIUM

The visitors were welcomed by slaves and shown into the atrium, a large entrance hall, where they waited to see their patron. The atrium was open to the sky, with an ornamental pool, called an impluvium, which collected rainwater. The statue of the faun was found here. The room's walls would have been lined with busts of the family's ancestors.

The atrium of the House of the Faun today, with a bronze copy of the original faun standing in the impluvium.

MEETING THE PATRON

Visitors were then called into the tablinum, an office to the side of the atrium, opposite the entrance of the house. It was open to the front, and divided from the atrium by curtains or screens. Here, the master of the house would receive his guests one by one.

You are standing in front of the tablinum, the office of the master of the House of the Faun. It looks out onto the first of two peristyles (courtyard gardens).

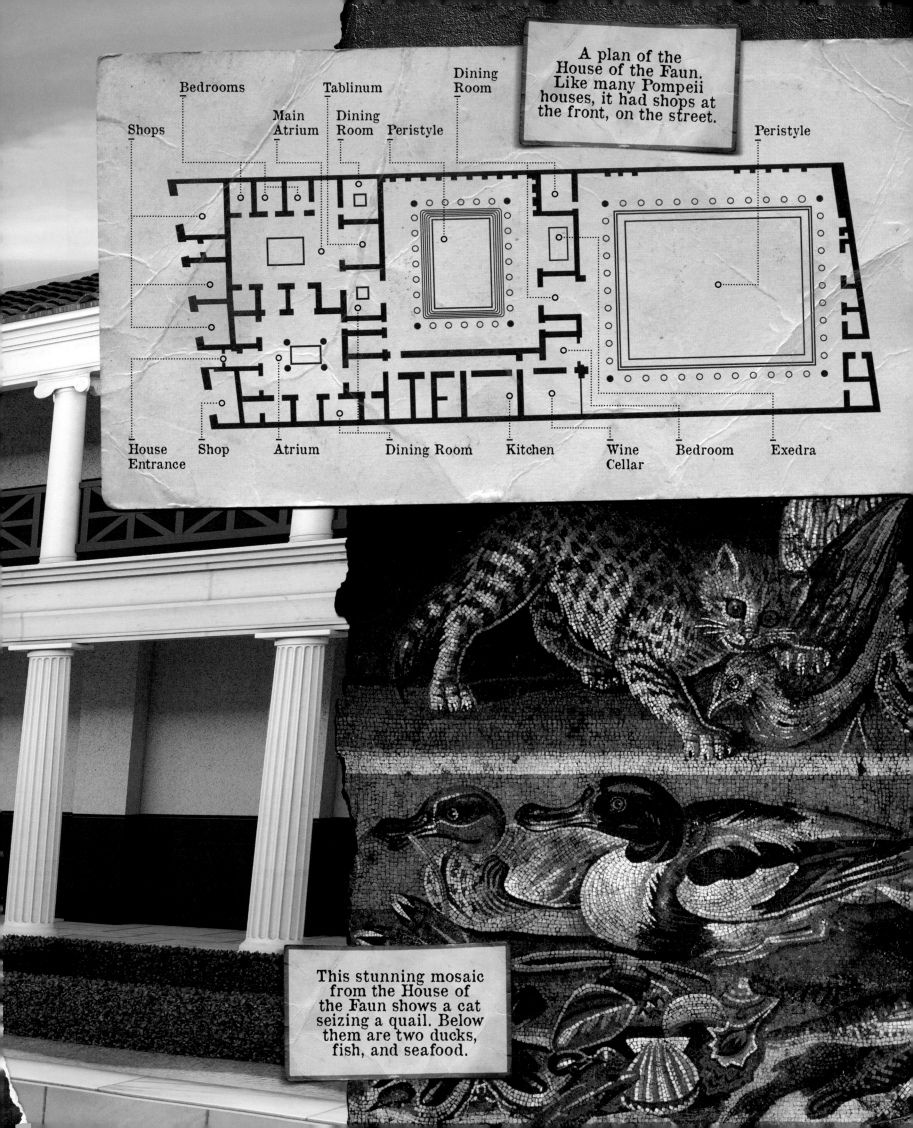

A plan of the House of the Faun. Like many Pompeii houses, it had shops at the front, on the street.

Bedrooms

Tablinum

Dining Room

Main Atrium

Shops

Dining Room

Peristyle

Peristyle

House Entrance

Shop

Atrium

Dining Room

Kitchen

Wine Cellar

Bedroom

Exedra

This stunning mosaic from the House of the Faun shows a cat seizing a quail. Below them are two ducks, fish, and seafood.

This wall painting from the Villa of Agrippa Postumus is decorated in the third style, combining a landscape painting with flat panels of color.

You are standing in a typical peristyle garden similar to the second peristyle of the House of the Faun. The House of the Faun was unusual in having two peristyles: most houses had one.

A DINING ROOM

The richer people of Pompeii had their main meal, called cena, in the late afternoon and evening, reclining on couches. A dinner party was an opportunity for the host to display wealth and taste. Guests would be impressed by expensive tableware and unusual dishes. There was often entertainment, such as acrobatics, music, or readings from a book.

Wealthy people from Pompeii ate from silver dinnerware, such as these serving dishes and jugs. Silver was highly prized by the Romans.

ROMAN MENU

Meals for wealthy Romans had several courses, beginning with a gustatio or starter, such as salads or shellfish. This was followed by the fercula ("dishes which are carried"), comprising up to seven meat and fish dishes. Foods were sweetened with honey and often heavily spiced. A favorite ingredient was a piquant sauce made from fermented fish intestines. Diners ate with their fingers or with a spoon. Slaves brought water to wash hands so the guests could wash their hands before the meal and between courses.

"LET WATER WASH YOUR FEET CLEAN AND A SLAVE WIPE THEM DRY; LET A CLOTH COVER THE COUCH; TAKE CARE OF OUR LINENS."
Writing on the wall of the dining room in the House of the Moralist

We can see how the Romans ate thanks to paintings like this one from the House of the Chaste Lovers.

This painting from Pompeii shows the end of a dinner party. A slave helps one guest with his shoes, while another slave supports a drunk guest who is sick!

THE TRICLINIUM

It was usual to have three couches in a dining room, or triclinium, arranged around a central table. The fourth side was left open so that slaves could serve the dishes. Often, the couches were made of stone, with cushions laid on top.

This triclinium, from the House of the Moralist, shows the arrangement of the couches, which sloped down to the wall behind.

TABLE ETIQUETTE

Places on the couches were arranged by status. The most important guest was positioned on the left side of the central couch. The host reclined on the right side of the left-hand couch. The couch on the right was for the lowest ranking guests. Diners leaned on their left elbows, eating with their right hands.

HOUSEHOLD TREASURES

Everyday objects and personal possessions discovered in the buried houses of Pompeii give valuable clues about Roman life. Discoveries range from hairpins to stashes of gold and silver found in larger houses, such as the House of Menander. Many look surprisingly like objects we use today.

This silver embossed mirror is one of many treasures from the House of Menander.

MIRROR, MIRROR

The House of Menander was one of the most magnificent houses in Pompeii. When it was excavated in 1930, a hoard of jewelry, gold and silver coins, and 118 silver vessels were discovered in a chest in the cellar. This gave the house its nickname, "the House of the Silverware."

This is the hearth from the kitchen of the House of the Vetti.

KITCHENS

Kitchens were dark, unadorned, and usually tucked away at the back of the house, for they were only seen by the slaves who worked there. The only permanent feature found in most kitchens is a masonry hearth with a tiled top and an arched recess underneath for storing fuel. Cooking was done on this open hearth, with pots set over burning charcoal or wood.

A bronze food warmer from the House of the Four Styles.

MOVABLE FEASTS

It's thought that bronze food warmers were used in grand dining rooms. A fire would have been lit underneath, and food inserted through small doors. In winter, these had the advantage of keeping the dinner guests warm, too.

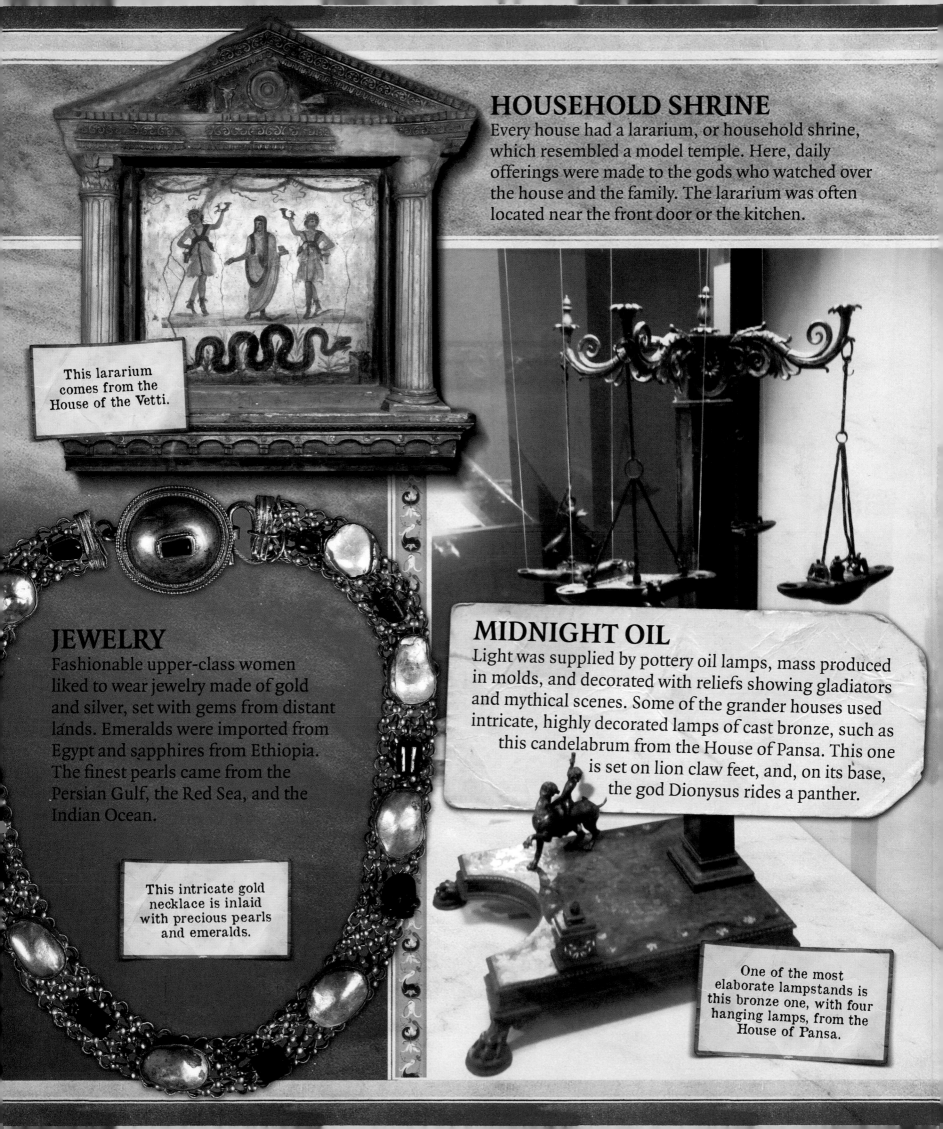

HOUSEHOLD SHRINE

Every house had a lararium, or household shrine, which resembled a model temple. Here, daily offerings were made to the gods who watched over the house and the family. The lararium was often located near the front door or the kitchen.

This lararium comes from the House of the Vetti.

JEWELRY

Fashionable upper-class women liked to wear jewelry made of gold and silver, set with gems from distant lands. Emeralds were imported from Egypt and sapphires from Ethiopia. The finest pearls came from the Persian Gulf, the Red Sea, and the Indian Ocean.

This intricate gold necklace is inlaid with precious pearls and emeralds.

MIDNIGHT OIL

Light was supplied by pottery oil lamps, mass produced in molds, and decorated with reliefs showing gladiators and mythical scenes. Some of the grander houses used intricate, highly decorated lamps of cast bronze, such as this candelabrum from the House of Pansa. This one is set on lion claw feet, and, on its base, the god Dionysus rides a panther.

One of the most elaborate lampstands is this bronze one, with four hanging lamps, from the House of Pansa.

GARDENS

The wealthy people of Pompeii loved gardens, which were laid out in an orderly way, with rows of columns, hedges, small statues, and fountains. A garden was often enclosed by a peristyle, a colonnaded walk that provided shade on hot days. Although no plants survived the volcanic eruption, their roots left spaces in the earth, which have been used to identify them.

OSCILLUM

Hanging between the columns of a peristyle, there would often be oscilla, marble discs that flashed in the sunlight as they spun in the breeze. Oscilla were often decorated with scenes from myths.

This piece of an oscillum shows the mythical Greek hero Hercules capturing a monstrous boar.

GARDEN PLANTS

Garden plants included small trees and shrubs, such as fig and olive trees. Flowers, such as roses, poppies (above), violets, and acanthus were popular for adding color.

The garden at the House of the Vetti has been replanted. It originally contained fountains, marble basins, and statues.

FLOWERS AND BIRDS

The Romans decorated their homes with paintings of garden scenes, featuring flowers and birds. When painted on garden walls, they made the garden seem bigger than it really was. In winter, when the real garden was mostly bare, the paintings were a reminder of spring.

A wall painting featuring a garden and birdbath decorated the walls of an outdoor dining room in the House of the Golden Bracelet.

THE FORUM

Welcome to the forum, the main square of Pompeii, and the bustling center of government, business, law, and religion. It was a popular meeting place, with the city's chief public buildings arranged around it. Most days it would have been crowded with stallholders, merchants, and politicians.

You are standing in the forum, looking northwest, toward the Temple of Jupiter. Built around 150 BCE, this tall temple was designed to dominate the forum.

Jupiter was the god of the sky and the protector of the state and its laws. In this statue, Jupiter is holding a lightning bolt.

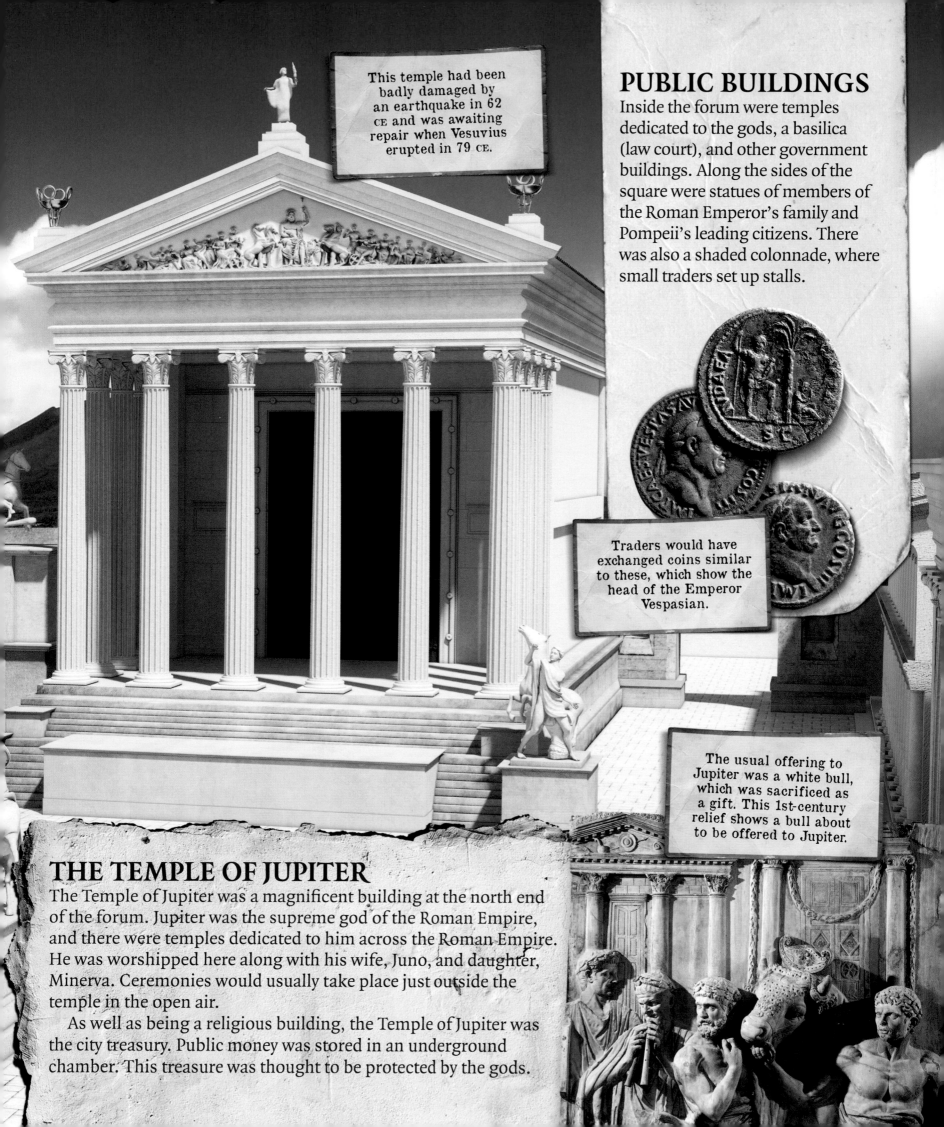

This temple had been badly damaged by an earthquake in 62 CE and was awaiting repair when Vesuvius erupted in 79 CE.

PUBLIC BUILDINGS

Inside the forum were temples dedicated to the gods, a basilica (law court), and other government buildings. Along the sides of the square were statues of members of the Roman Emperor's family and Pompeii's leading citizens. There was also a shaded colonnade, where small traders set up stalls.

Traders would have exchanged coins similar to these, which show the head of the Emperor Vespasian.

The usual offering to Jupiter was a white bull, which was sacrificed as a gift. This 1st-century relief shows a bull about to be offered to Jupiter.

THE TEMPLE OF JUPITER

The Temple of Jupiter was a magnificent building at the north end of the forum. Jupiter was the supreme god of the Roman Empire, and there were temples dedicated to him across the Roman Empire. He was worshipped here along with his wife, Juno, and daughter, Minerva. Ceremonies would usually take place just outside the temple in the open air.

As well as being a religious building, the Temple of Jupiter was the city treasury. Public money was stored in an underground chamber. This treasure was thought to be protected by the gods.

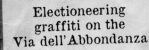

A MEETING PLACE

The elections, in which only male citizens could vote, took place in the forum, in a big hall called the comitium. Here, the men of Pompeii chose the magistrates (officials) who ran their town. The streets of Pompeii were covered with election slogans, which shows how important politics was to the local people.

"ALL OF THE FRUIT SELLERS URGE THE ELECTION OF M. HOLCONIUS PRISCUS AS DUUMVIR."

Election slogan painted on a wall

Merchants would have used scales similar to these bronze ones to weigh their goods.

THE MACELLUM

In the forum's northeast corner, there was a macellum, a covered food market. It had a fish market in the center and a small enclosure where live sheep were kept—sold to be sacrificed. It also traded wine and oil.

This beautiful Mediterranean fish mosaic was discovered in a house in Pompeii. Fish such as these were sold at the macellum.

MAGISTRATES

The most important officials were two duumvirs ("two men"), who administered justice and oversaw meetings of the town council. There were also two aediles, junior magistrates who maintained public buildings. Both duumvirs and aediles were elected annually.

EUMACHIA

Although women did not vote, they played an important role in the life of the town. The Building of Eumachia, one of the largest in the forum, was built by a rich woman called Eumachia. She was a priestess of Venus and a patroness of the cloth trade. Her building may have been an auction house, warehouse, or meeting place for cloth merchants.

BASILICA

The basilica, built around 130–120 BCE, was the oldest building in Pompeii. Measuring 215 by 79 feet (65 by 24 m), the basilica served as the law court, where the duumvirs oversaw trials. It was also a place where businessmen met to make deals.

Inside the grand basilica building, there was a colonnade of 25 brick columns.

"I'LL SHOW YOU WHERE TO FIND ALL SORTS OF MEN, GOOD OR BAD OR HONEST MEN OR RASCALS"

A description of the forum of Rome by playwright Plautus (254–184 BCE)

A guild of cloth merchants erected this statue of Eumachia in the veiled form of a priestess.

A BAR

There are around 150 bars in Pompeii, mostly on main streets, with many near the city's gates. They can be identified thanks to their brightly painted masonry counters. Set into them were large pottery jars, called dolia. These dolia were used to store dry food, such as beans and vegetables. Food was cooked in a pan over a stove at the back of the room. Bars were mostly used by the poor, who did not have kitchens in their homes.

ASELLINA'S BAR

Asellina's Bar is one of the best preserved in Pompeii. When it was excavated, its terracotta and bronze vessels were all found on the counter. The day's petty cash was also found in the remains of a bag in one of the dolia. Asellina was one of several women's names written on the bar's wall. These were probably the waitresses.

You are standing in front of Asellina's Bar. Customers eat and drink standing at the counter. A wooden staircase at the back of the bar leads to rooms above.

This terracotta vessel in the form of a cockerel was one of the items found in Asellina's Bar.

GAMBLING

Some of the larger bars had masonry tables and benches, where drinkers passed their time gambling with dice. Dice have been found in several of the bars.

PAINTED SHRINE

Vetutius Placidus' Bar had a painted shrine showing Mercury, god of trade, and Bacchus, god of wine. These were the most important gods for a bar owner. In the center, you can see the genius, or guardian spirit of the owner, flanked by two lares, household gods.

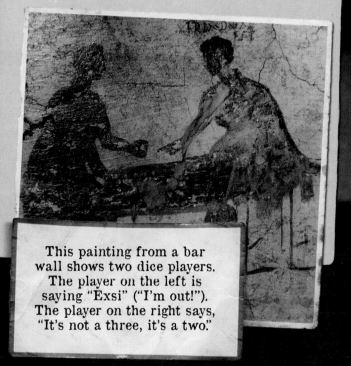

This painting from a bar wall shows two dice players. The player on the left is saying "Exsi" ("I'm out!"). The player on the right says, "It's not a three, it's a two."

The painted shrine from the Vetutius Placidus' Bar. You can see Mercury (far left), Bacchus (far right), and the guardian spirit (center).

A FULLONICA

Pompeii had eleven fullonicae (fulleries), which played the final role in the manufacture of cloth and also acted as laundries, where wealthy Romans sent their clothes to be cleaned. Like other trades, the fullers had their own collegia, or guild. Members gathered to celebrate festivals in honor of their patron goddess, Minerva, or to offer support for candidates in elections.

"SULPHUR IS USED FOR FUMIGATING WOOL, A PROCESS WHICH CONTRIBUTES VERY GREATLY TO MAKING THE WOOL WHITE AND SOFT."

Pliny the Elder, Natural History

This painting from a Pompeii fullonica shows children and an adult treading cloth in basins.

CLEANING THE CLOTH

The first stage in cleaning cloth was to soak it in urine. This was collected in pots, left in the street for passersby to pee into. The cloth was then washed and stamped on in bronze basins containing water and fuller's earth, a clay that absorbed grease. A wall painting shows that this job was often done by children, probably slaves.

RINSING

The next stage was to rinse the cloth in fresh water. Fullonicae are easy to recognize because of the large tanks, which were used for the process. Fresh water flowed from tank to tank. Fullonicae used huge amounts of water.

BLEACHING

The fullers bleached white cloth by spreading it over a basketlike frame on top of burning sulphur. Because of the acrid smell produced by sulphur, this was done in the open air, on the roof. Although no frames survive, there is a painting of a man carrying one on the wall of the Veranius Hypsaeus' Fullonica.

This painting shows a fuller carrying his bleaching frame and a pot of sulphur. The owl perched on top is sacred to Minerva, patroness of fullers.

This painting from a fullonica shows a press with two metal screws mounted in a wooden frame.

PRESSING

The last stage was to press the cloth flat. The clean cloth was placed between two wooden plates and then squeezed together by pressure applied from upright screws at the top of the press. The screw press, also used in wine and olive oil production, was a Roman invention.

This is one of the water tanks from Stephanus' Fullonica, which was a converted house.

A BAKERY

So far, 33 bakeries have been found in Pompeii. These have ovens and tall mills, which were operated by donkeys or mules. Five mule skeletons were found in one bakery. The bakers of Pompeii were involved in the whole bread-making process, from grinding the grain to make flour to kneading dough and baking bread. Like the fullers, the bakers had their own trade guild.

This relief from a baker's sarcophagus (stone coffin) shows a horse-operated mill. The donkeys and mules of Pompeii were harnessed and blinkered just like this horse.

GRINDING

The grain was ground in tall mills made of volcanic stone. The upper stone would be turned by a pair of donkeys or mules, chained on each side. They wore blinkers over their eyes to prevent them from being distracted. Grain was poured in at the top and the flour collected on the circular base.

OVENS

Roman ovens were made of brick and were similar to modern pizza ovens. A wood or charcoal fire was burned inside to heat them. When the temperature was hot enough, the fire was raked out, and the loaves baked in the ashes.

This mosaic shows a baker placing bread in the oven using a long wooden paddle, like those still used in pizzerias today.

You are standing in a typical Pompeian bakery. You can see the tall mills, and the paved floor, to prevent wear and tear on the donkeys' hooves.

One bakery oven was found with 81 well-preserved loaves still inside. Each was divided into eight segments for easy tearing.

THE STABIAN BATHS

Pompeii, like every Roman town, had thermae, or public baths, which were visited by rich and poor alike. A bathhouse was much more than a place to wash. It was like a leisure center, with places for exercise and relaxation. Pompeii had three large public baths. We shall visit the biggest of them, the Stabian Thermae.

HEATING SYSTEM

Rooms in the baths were heated to different temperatures, using an underfloor heating system, called a hypocaust. Hot air passed through spaces beneath the floors, which were raised on brick columns, and within the walls. The rooms nearest the furnace were the hottest. The caldarium here would have been full of steam, but another type of hot room, a laconicum, offered dry heat, like a sauna.

You are standing in the men's caldarium, the hot steam room, of the Stabian Baths, looking toward the cold water fountain. At the other end of the room was a heated pool.

THE CALDARIUM

Visitors to the baths would start off in the warm tepidarium room then walk through to the hotter caldarium. The floor of a caldarium would be so hot that visitors had to wear wooden clogs. After working up a sweat, they might splash themselves with cold water from the fountain to cool down.

The underfloor hypocaust heating system of the Stabian Baths. Hot air generated by a furnace was circulated underground.

"I LIVE RIGHT ABOVE THE PUBLIC
BATHS. IMAGINE THE KINDS OF NOISE I
HAVE TO PUT UP WITH! THERE ARE THE
ENERGETIC TYPES, HEAVING WEIGHTS
ABOUT WITH GRUNTS AND GASPS ...
AND THE PEOPLE WHO LEAP INTO THE
POOL WITH A TREMENDOUS SPLASH."

Seneca, *On Noise*, c60 CE

THE PALAESTRA

The Stabian Baths had a large open area, called a palaestra, used for exercising. People could run, lift weights, wrestle, and play ball games here. Before exercising, they rubbed their bodies with scented olive oil.

You are standing in the palaestra, a large exercise area, looking toward the swimming pool. Elaborate wall paintings adorned the walls.

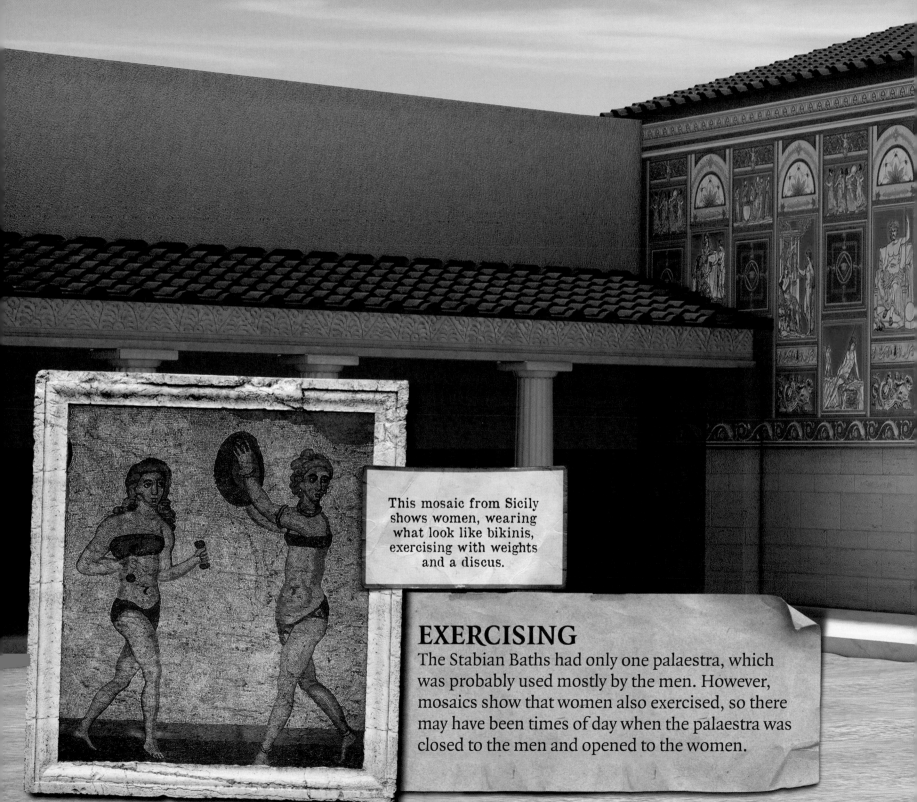

This mosaic from Sicily shows women, wearing what look like bikinis, exercising with weights and a discus.

EXERCISING

The Stabian Baths had only one palaestra, which was probably used mostly by the men. However, mosaics show that women also exercised, so there may have been times of day when the palaestra was closed to the men and opened to the women.

USING THE BATHS

The people of Pompeii would typically visit the Stabian Baths in the afternoon, after a morning's work, if they were able. The baths were a place not just for exercise and washing, but also socializing, gossiping, and making business deals.

CHANGING ROOMS

At the Stabian Baths, there were separate entrances for men and women and different sections for male and female bathing. On arrival at the Stabian Baths, visitors first undressed, leaving their clothes in the apodyterium (undressing room). Slaves watched over belongings, but theft was still common.

This is the women's apodyterium from the Stabian Baths. The niches in the walls were places for the women to leave their clothes. The steps lead up to a cold plunge pool.

THE TOILETS

The Stabian Baths also included toilets where people sat side by side on long rows of wooden seats. Instead of toilet paper, they would clean themselves with a sea sponge on a stick, which would then be rinsed in a channel of water that flowed at their feet.

Communal Roman toilets at the archeological site of Ostia Antica, just outside Rome.

This painting showing a girl having her hair dressed comes from the palaestra of a bathhouse in Herculaneum.

BATH ART

A bathhouse was like an art gallery, with statues and wall paintings. For the poor people of Pompeii, the baths would be one of the most luxurious buildings they would ever enter.

Roman strigils and tweezers (right) and a manicure set (bottom left).

STRIGIL AND OIL

After exercising, bathers would have the oil and sweat scraped from their bodies using a curved bronze strigil. This would be done, usually by slaves, in the destrictarium, or scraping room. The poorest, who did not have slaves, would take turns to scrape each other.

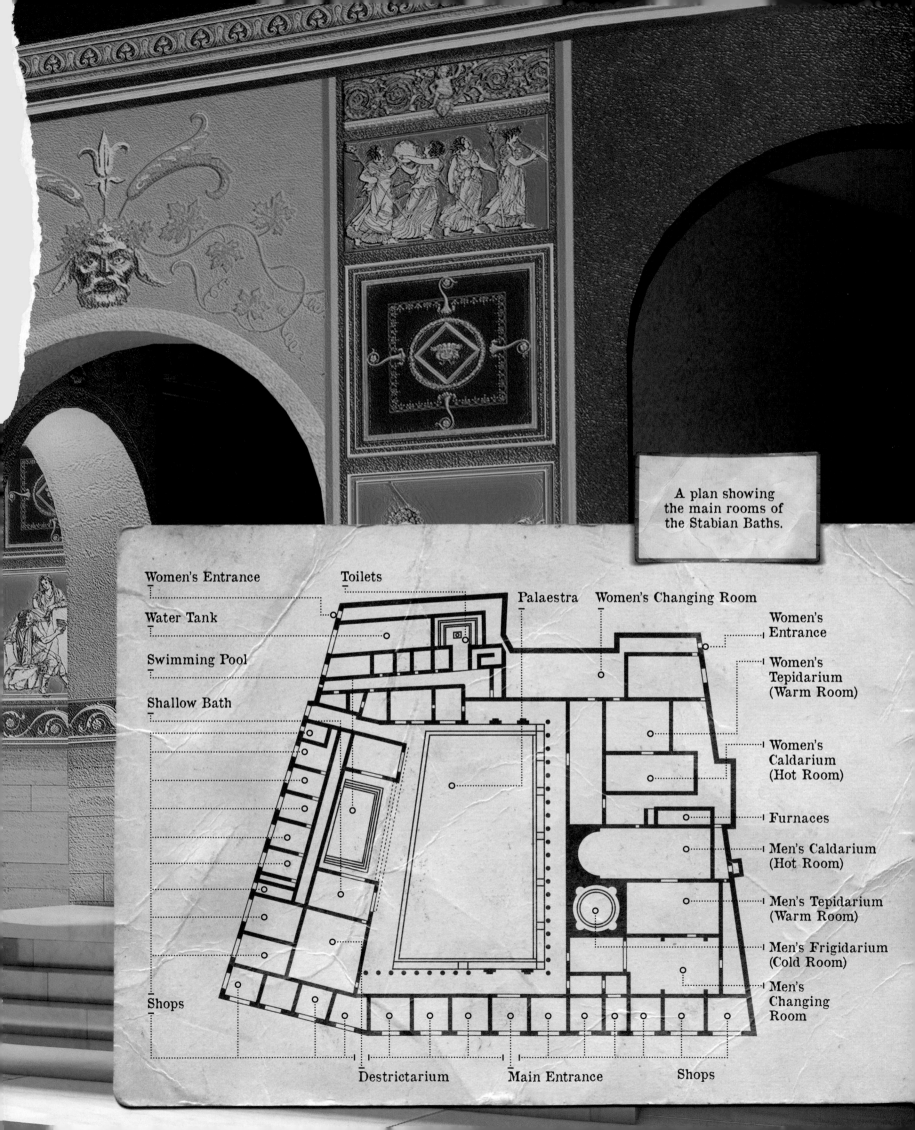

A plan showing the main rooms of the Stabian Baths.

Women's Entrance

Water Tank

Swimming Pool

Shallow Bath

Toilets

Palaestra

Women's Changing Room

Women's Entrance

Women's Tepidarium (Warm Room)

Women's Caldarium (Hot Room)

Furnaces

Men's Caldarium (Hot Room)

Men's Tepidarium (Warm Room)

Men's Frigidarium (Cold Room)

Men's Changing Room

Shops

Destrictarium

Main Entrance

Shops

SWIMMING POOL

At the west end of the palaestra was a large unheated swimming pool where the visitors could take a dip after exercising. To the side of the pool was a shallow bath, which bathers walked through to clean their feet before plunging into the pool.

THE WATER SUPPLY

A vast amount of water was needed in Pompeii—for the public baths, houses, gardens, street fountains, and public latrines. It's been estimated that 1,684,800 gallons (6,480,000 l) of water flowed into the city every day. The water was brought along a great aqueduct, or water channel, from springs in the mountains of Campania. The whole aqueduct, which flowed mostly underground, was around 87 miles (140 km) long, and supplied all the nearby towns.

"I ASK YOU! JUST COMPARE THE VAST MONUMENTS OF THIS VITAL AQUEDUCT SYSTEM WITH THOSE USELESS PYRAMIDS OR THE GOOD-FOR-NOTHING TOURIST ATTRACTIONS OF THE GREEKS."

Frontinus, On Aqueducts

WATER DISTRIBUTOR

On entering Pompeii, the water flowed into a large brick castellum aquae (water distributor). It was filtered through a metal mesh, and then separated into three pipes, one each for street fountains, public buildings, such as baths, and private houses. If water supplies fell low, private houses had their water cut off before the public fountains.

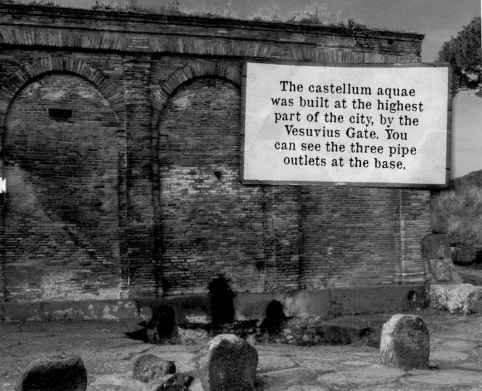

The castellum aquae was built at the highest part of the city, by the Vesuvius Gate. You can see the three pipe outlets at the base.

This is the piscina mirabilis, a great cistern, where the aqueduct ended at a port along the coast called Misenum.

CITY DRAINS

Because Pompeii was an old city, it had no underground sewers, unlike more modern towns, such as neighboring Herculaneum. The streets of Pompeii acted as a drainage system, with sewage from latrines flowing along them. This was constantly flushed by the overflowing water from the street fountains and bathhouses.

People used stepping stones to cross the streets, which flowed with sewage and water. Ruts enabled carts to avoid hitting the stones.

STREET FOUNTAINS

There were 40 street fountains, spaced at regular 330 foot (100 m) distances around the city, often located at street corners. Each had a large basin beneath a spout decorated with a carving, such as a griffin, cockerel, horn of plenty, or the face of a god.

The face of the god Mercury, who can be recognized by his winged hat, decorates a water fountain.

THE THEATRE

Pompeii had two stone theatres on the south side of the city. There was a large, open air theatre, which could seat more than 4,000 people, and a small roofed theatre, which held around 1,200. While the larger one staged plays, the smaller one was mainly used for musical performances. Graffiti praising star actors shows us that the theatre was popular.

OPEN AIR THEATRE

The large theatre was built on the side of a hill during the 2nd century BCE. At the back of the stage, there would originally have been a tall "skene" building, where the actors changed their costumes. It served as the setting for the play, and is the origin of our own word, "scene."

The large theatre, which has been restored, is still used for theatrical performances.

"HERE'S TO ACTIUS, COME BACK TO YOUR PEOPLE SOON."

Graffito praising the pantomime actor Actius Anicetus

SHOW TIME!

There were several different types of play. Alongside Greek tragedy and comedy, there was an Italian form called the Atellan Farce. It featured regular characters, such as Manducus, the glutton, and Bucco, the boaster. The most popular type was the pantomime, which resembled ballet. Accompanied by musicians, a single star actor, wearing various masks, acted out a story from a myth using only body movements.

For most types of theatre, the actors wore masks, like the two in this mosaic. These would have been worn in a comedy.

These actors are about to perform a Greek satyr play, playing the wild goatish companions of Bacchus, the wine god.

ACTORS

This mosaic, from the House of the Tragic Poet, shows actors preparing to go onstage. You can see their large masks, a piper, and an actor being helped into his costume.

MUSICIANS

Another mosaic, from the Villa of Cicero, shows masked musicians, who play an aulos (double pipe), castanets, and a big tambourine. This is thought to be a scene from a comedy by Menander, a 4th century BCE Greek playwright.

This mosaic showing musicians was made by a Greek artist, Dioskourides of Samos.

You are standing in the amphitheatre of Pompeii, looking up toward the raised rows of seats. Two thousand years ago, vast crowds gathered here to watch gladiators, who were slaves or criminals, fight to the death.

RIOT!

A wall painting from a house in Pompeii shows a riot that took place in the amphitheatre in 59 CE. Fighting broke out between Pompeians and visitors from the neighboring town of Nuceria. Many Nucerians were killed or wounded. The Nucerians complained to Emperor Nero, who banned amphitheatre shows in Pompeii for ten years.

The painting of the riot in the amphitheatre also shows the awning that shielded the crowd from the sun.

THE AMPHITHEATRE

The most popular entertainment in Pompeii was not theatre, but gladiator and wild beast shows. These were staged in the amphitheatre ("double theatre"), built in the southeastern corner of the town. Built in about 70 BCE, Pompeii's is one of the world's oldest surviving amphitheatres. It could seat 20,000 people, which is more than the whole population of the city. Its size shows that people came from all over the region to see the shows.

WILD BEASTS

Wild animals, trapped in great numbers in North Africa and the Middle East, were shipped to Italy to be exhibited in amphitheatres. These included lions, bears, elephants, and ostriches. They were hunted by gladiators called bestiarii.

Wild animals were also used to execute criminals, another form of entertainment exhibited in amphitheatres.

A REAL FIGHT

A sketch found in Pompeii shows a real fight that took place in the amphitheatre. The writing over the dueling gladiators says, "Hilarus, Neronian, fought 14, 12 victories, victor. Creunus, fought 7, 5 victories, reprieved."

The sketch shows that fights took place to the accompaniment of music.

THE GLADIATORS

There were around 20 types of gladiator, each with his own distinctive weapons, armor, and style of combat. Spectators also had their favorite kind of fighter, and liked to watch contests between different types. It was exciting to watch a fast, lightly armed fighter, such as a retiarus, fighting a better protected but slower gladiator.

THE BARRACKS

The gladiators lived in a large barracks on the south side of the town. In one room, several skeletons have been found where gladiators died at the time of the eruption. Gladiators were mostly free to come and go, and some were treated like celebrities. The barrack walls are covered with graffiti, written by the gladiators themselves. They boasted about their victories and their popularity with the women of Pompeii.

This helmet, found in the gladitorial barracks, belonged to a type of gladiator called a thracian. The griffin on top was a mythical animal associated with Thrace.

The barracks had a large open palaestra (exercise area) where the gladiators trained.

"CELADUS THE THRACIAN, THE GLORY OF THE GIRLS, WHO MAKES ALL THE GIRLS SIGH."

Graffiti from the barracks in Pompeii

RETIARUS

The retiarus (net man) was armed like a fisherman, with a trident, a three-pronged fishing spear, and a weighted net. He threw the net over his opponent to trap him, and then speared him with his trident. Speed was important for a retiarus, so he wore no armor other than a manica, or shoulder guard, on his left arm.

SECUTOR

The retiarus often fought a secutor (pursuer). He had a smooth egg-shaped helmet, designed so that it would not get trapped in the retiarus' net. It covered his whole face, apart from two small eyeholes. He carried a sword and a long shield and wore a manica on his right arm and a greave (guard) on his left leg.

THRACIAN

A thracian had armor and weapons based on Rome's traditional enemies in Thrace (modern Bulgaria). Like a real Thracian, he had a small curved sword called a sica and a small shield. But his elaborate helmet, with a huge crest topped by a griffin, was unlike anything worn in real warfare. It was designed for display in the amphitheatre.

This mosaic shows a retiarus (left) stabbing a secutor (right) with his trident.

HOPLOMACHUS

A thracian was often paired with a more heavily armored hoplomachus ("armed fighter" in Greek). He wore shin guards and an arm guard on his sword arm, and crouched behind a long curved shield. He had a wide brimmed helmet decorated with feathers.

This lamp shows a wounded hoplomachus. The gladiator on the left is a type called a samnite.

A 2nd century mosaic depicting different types of gladiators. A referee stands third from the right.

POMPEII TODAY

Pompeii is one of the most popular tourist sites in the world, and every year over two million visitors explore the ruins of the ancient town.

THE FUTURE

Although they provide money that helps to maintain the site, the tourists also damage the site through wear and tear. The ruins are also exposed to rain, pigeon droppings, sunlight, which makes paintings fade, and even deliberate vandalism.

In March 2014, many walls in Pompeii collapsed following heavy rainfall. The Italian government held an emergency meeting, releasing 2.6 million Euros for urgent repair work.

Although much of the city is still unexcavated, the director, Pietro Giovanni Guzzo, has called a temporary halt on further excavation. The aim now is to preserve what has been exposed so everyone can continue to enjoy the wonders of this fascinating city.

The ruins of the Pompeii forum with Mt. Vesuvius in the background. Vesuvius last erupted in 1944 and may yet erupt in the future.